Cinnamon Clouds

Cinnamon Clouds

LINDA WILKINSON

HARVEST HOUSE PUBLISHERS
Irvine, California 92714

Copyright©1979 by Harvest House Publishers
Irvine, California 92714

Library of Congress Catalog Card Number: 78-55222
ISBN: 0-89081-139-3

PRINTED IN THE UNITED STATES OF AMERICA

Design and photos: Koechel Design, Minneapolis, Minnesota
Cover photo: Ed Arness

Contents

Cinnamon Clouds

Cinnamon clouds are melting in the sky—
they're raining their special music on people who pass by.
To be kissed by a cinnamon cloud creates magic
like the waving of a wand—
turns a frog into a prince
as he floats upon his pond.
Your imagination can carry you to a land where love is in the air
and billowy cinnamon clouds are floating everywhere.
It is your privilege to believe in dreams come true—
to sit upon a water lily and relish the wealth of your view.

If your mind can become as that of a little child,
there will be no end to the possibilities
that your mind will compile—
for realities are dreams come true
and a way of showing God's love to you.
He is the maker of cinnamon clouds—
His children are the recipients, and He waits for the sound of
"Thank You—I believe I am found."

For The Love Of Children

For the love of children,
you opened our eyes to the vision
of tiny hearts as they run along at Your side.
You've helped us to understand
that the answer was not the rule of an iron hand—
but an unmistakable spirit of compassion.
As we learned to love the ways of infants to teens,
we felt Your hands guiding our lives
with the years in between.

Lord, You know we didn't pray together every day,
and our time for devotions
was usually taken up with play—
but, oh, how we loved each other.
We haven't lived by all the rules,
but we've survived a dozen disasters or more—
and now we have the time to adventurously explore
the world with our children.
They talk to us from dawn to night
about everything from love and sex
to the almighty powers that You possess—
and for the love of our children,
You know we did our best.

Never
A Stranger

A stranger has never walked through my door,
nor have I ever met one on the street.
The strength of compatible minds
can entwine the spirits of lonely souls.
I would like to have you for a friend
and do for you what I know you would do for me,
and as I entertain you I can clearly see—
that in caring for you I have cared for the Son of God,
and within this theory there is no fraud.
For as He is, so are we, never strangers—
just people set free from the bonds
of circumstance and formality.
Come on in and sit for a while,
and talk of the goodness that life can lend—
never a stranger, always a friend.

Jesus Passed By Here

Jesus passed by here today,
and in the course of His journey
I felt I was watching an instant replay—
of so many times in the midst of my life
when I somehow believed He had vanished from my sight—
and then there would be a phone call or a knock on the door.
It would sound familiar—I had heard it before.
The clothes were not His and certainly not the voice—
yet I felt the urgency of the message, I had no other choice.
For when Jesus passes by, He's in many forms and styles—
and He is no respecter of men or of miles.

He goes where He's needed, whether it's the finest hotel
or the dingiest dark hole of hell.
It was great to hear His voice today
though it came through someone else —
the knowledge of His presence was ever so powerfully felt.
It may be that He will pass by your house tomorrow
and join in with your laughter or feel the depth of your sorrow —
but one thing is for sure, love everyone you see
for you may not be aware of just who it will be.
For Jesus is international, and He's powerful,
and He would not pass you by
unless you chose to close your door
to the loneliness in some stranger's eyes.

Destruction

What do I do when my heart is so full of joy
that I can scarcely contain it in my being—
and then all of a sudden the phone rings
and one of my friends approaches me with the fact
that I am not doing what I should be doing?
"Didn't you know
that there's a new seminar on marriage
you should be attending,
classes on child development
that you should be auditing
and a new program on making friends
that you should be following?"
Well now—isn't it strange
that my joyful spirit is diminishing,
that my stomach is churning and my heart is burning?

Lord, can't they see
that not everyone fits into the same mold
or walks the same road?
I've been through the seminars, classes and books.
My husband is loved, my children are cherished,
and I've learned to improve on my looks.
Now, if I could have a few years
just to enjoy the essence of life—
to add to it, to take from it and most of all to share it—
then, who knows, maybe I'll be teaching
some of those very helpful classes of instruction,
but Lord, don't let me ever promote it
to the point of causing destruction.

A Sense Of Love

There are cinnamon sticks growing in my backyard,
and out among the trees there's a fragrance
of apple blossoms, and it smells like love to me.
I cuddle soft baby kittens, and my heart is being warmed
by my children with their kisses, and it feels like love.
From my bedroom window I can hear a carnival—
it's summertime, and everything is vibrantly alive—
and the echoes coming forth are as sweet as the sounds
of honey in a beehive, and I can hear love.

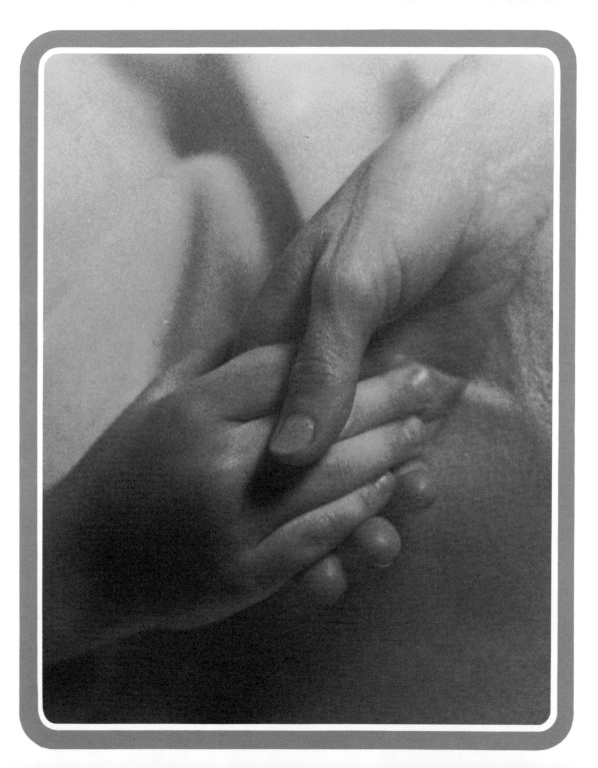

Blankets of soft velvet, warm human hands,
toasted English muffins and hugs that were unplanned—
I have tasted of love.
Create in your heart a picture of God
as He gathers all the ones you hold dear
and takes their hands along with yours
and forms a world without fear.
As He cares for you and clothes your mind
like the warmth of a glove—
you will have completely known the meaning of love.

The Devil's Zoo

You picked me up,
out of a vast wasteland of floundering souls.
You sat me on Your knee,
and ever so gently You showed me eternity.
I knew it wasn't so long in coming
but it would be long-lasting,
and was I to spend it with You—
or casually jump on the bandwagon
bound for the devil's zoo?
In a twinkling I could see
that my only real hope was in the security
of sitting right here on Your knee.
But Jesus, I just want to look over the side
and see where that wagon is heading—
and I promise I won't ask for anything more.

Then before I knew it
I had jumped right on board,
and You didn't pick me up—
I didn't know You as Lord.
I got my fill of treasure-packed lives
(they were all so carefully clothed
in an angel's disguise),
and just about the time that the pickup was due,
I was surprisingly picked up by You.
Today, as I'm safe in Your arms,
if there's any way to reach those in disguise,
give me the courage to love through Your eyes.
Just maybe we can pick up a few of the souls
that are floundering in the devil's zoo.

Broken Heart

There has never been a broken heart He could not heal.
There has never been a withered spirit
that within His arms did not once again feel.
His patience and love far surpass that of any earthly source,
and His forgiveness is the glue
that binds the cuts of sorrow and remorse.
There has never been a temptation
that He did not experience first.
He must have felt the rage of those who resented His birth,
but there has never been any condemnation falling from His lips,
for there is no healing process in the words
"What have you done?"
He was born the Son of God—but human in every respect,
so He could walk the same road I would walk
and know firsthand just what to expect.
He is the only experienced physician
to handle the case before Him now.
I'm not just sure which remedy He will use,
but I can tell from reading His chart—
He has the only glue available to mend a broken heart.

I Love You

"I love you" is the message from my heart to yours.
My words will never be devoid of feeling or compassion,
for I have been there—
in your world of heartache and division.
My name is Jesus.
I have wept because people
did not understand or care
about the miracles they were observing
or the spirit of love drifting in the air.
I have been perplexed when sins were not forgiven
by my children who claimed me as their God—
yet they had no compassion for their so-called friends
whom they thought might be odd.

My heart has been saddened
when I have had to walk the road alone—
not seeing a friendly smile,
not having a place to call my own.
I have seen tragedy, I have felt hurt,
I have known the sting of death—
it was promised from my birth.
All the hurts of your life I've wrapped in mine—
I'm the lily of your valley, I'm the nectar in the vine.
All of this understanding I freely give to you—
if I can just hear you say "I love You, too."

Attachment

To be attached to people and things
is not in style these days.
Well then, why do I feel the need
to pour out my love
or the need to receive your praise?
It may be uncalled for,
but I could lure a thousand people through my door
if they could be told they were loved.
Maybe they could feel the strings of their hearts
being pulled instead of shoved.
I like to study the looks on the faces of my friends
when I can honestly tell them
that without them I would be chained in a den of misery.
Alone may be in style, but it will never take the place
of gathering in your arms the crying human race.
Attachments are not just vacuums—
they're for you and for me.
They are the life blood that controls our destinies—
for without each other we would drown
in love that was never used—
and create our own vacuum of never-ending blues.

A Little Love Thrown In

I think I needed a great big hug
with an "I love you" thrown in for good measure.
In all the world, I know there is no greater treasure.
What happened to the freedom that we need—
just to feel, to be able to express
a positive human emotion—
and to believe with our innermost being that it's real?
Why are we afraid of touching human lives—
is it easier to play the games and wear the disguise?
I love easily, but I play games, too—
after all, that's what I've been taught to do.

If I were to display a warm, friendly hug
with an "I love you" thrown in—
I might experience the judgment and conclusion
that I had sinned.
Well, you can have your games and masks of disguise,
but as for me, I cannot live with the fear
that I'll be misunderstood.
There must be a place where it will do someone good
just to feel wanted with "I love you" thrown in—
without the fear that they might have committed
some unforgivable sin.

I Choose Love

What do you think is wrong with our youth today—
did they get too much hell-fire and brimstone
when some love should have been openly displayed?
It might be hard to understand,
but the vices of a past generation
are causing a separation among people today—
and I do remember reading that Christ is the author
of peace, not of confusion and doubt;
and believe me, too much hell-fire and brimstone
can cancel that out.
What is the need to be pushed and plodded down
by a guilt-ridden fellow man
when he himself cannot take a stand?

I can't live in the valleys created by tumbling stones
from the hell and fire erupting
from someone else's bones,
so I'll choose love; and I choose well, for I can't live
in an underestimated spell from a guilt-ridden cause.
I need to love You, Lord, and then love myself,
and after these needs are met there is nothing else—
for You've taken care of it all.
I believe that's the last time I will ever hear
the stones fall.

Reach The People

Reach out to the people
and they'll reach out for you.
Embrace their spirits and you'll gaze
upon their minds with a different view.
If you can show love to the people in the streets,
you will have broken down the wall
that you built against life's defeats.
If you will open your arms and give forth some love,
you could be surprised—
the joy will be something
you had thought impossible,
and you'll be a star in someone else's eyes.
If you can touch your friends with understanding
and give a bit of your time to strangers in need,
you may be wealthier than you think,
for you have learned how to feed the people.
You have reached out, now take the reward.
The warmth of human arms is greater
than any two-edged sword.

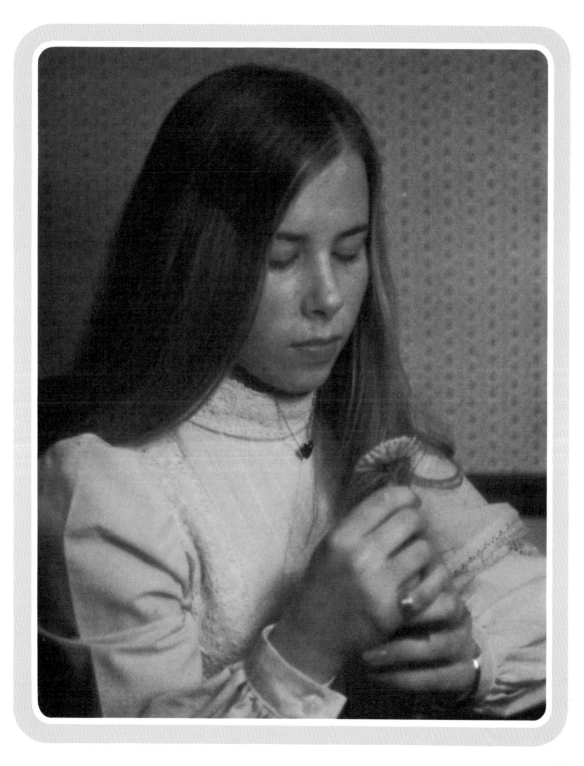

Good Morning, Son

Did I tell you that I think you're special
and more than I could have ever hoped for?
Did I ever let you know
that I'm proud of those muscles?
But I think 15 pounds of weight is enough
for you to be lifting this time around.
I think I forgot to kiss you goodnight,
but there's always another day—
and, Son, please remember to clean your room,
and don't forget to pray.
You're so handsome,
and you're displaying it extremely well
at the age of eleven—
but what am I going to do
when you grow beyond five foot seven?

Good morning, Son, it's another day.
It seems I have to reach to the sky
just to kiss you good-by.
I don't know if you've cleaned your room—
but I somehow believe that you've grown as tall
in your spirit as you have in my eyes,
and you know what, the room was unimportant;
and when you forgot to pray, I did it for you.
Oh, I hope you had enough time to play,
and I guess I just want to say
Thank you for being my son.

First A Mother

From the day that I met her I knew
that she was a mother first
and everything else came second.
Cradled in her arms was a beautiful, blond little girl,
and even as I inquired about her
she told me she was expecting another.
I have closely watched her life in the last few months,
and nothing has ever made a greater impression
than the love she possesses for her unborn child.
She never had a day that came easy
and never a night without pain;
and I have to say that once in a while
I did hear her complain, but even in those moments
she never lost that joy of counting every second,
just waiting for the birth of her baby girl or boy.
Lord, she deserves the best,
for she certainly has been put to the test.
She's a mother first, a jewel that's hard to find—
and I have no doubt
that her children are the treasures in her mind.

Mother's Best Friend

I remember her as something of a legend—
certainly she altered the course of my life.
Her eyes were maybe the bluest I had ever seen,
and they always twinkled with a friendly gleam.
She must have had her faults—but I couldn't find them.
All I seem to remember is kindness—
but then for her I had that special kind of love
that produces blindness—for faults that is.
I can still taste that creamy grapenut ice cream
that she produced from the refrigerator
whenever we came to visit.

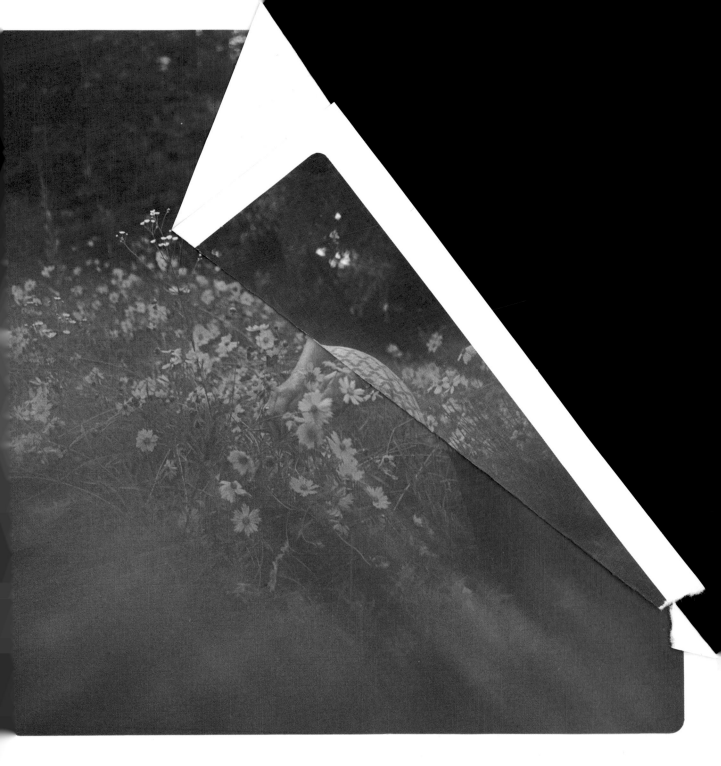

her own two hands,
was not to be had.
ing that old, round oatmeal box
he most beautiful doll cradles

ning I came across
apron that she made for me—
aybe three.
you believe, I walked through a home today
surprise one of her watercolor paintings
fore my eyes.
ved to write poetry, too.
thing she could do, she would do for you.
e was my mother's best friend for just about fifty years,
out Mother, did you know that at her death—
I also shed some tears?

The Mask

What would qualify me to be Your friend?
You would never expect perfection,
but You have no tolerance for sin.
It would be easy to make You happy—
just put my best foot forward,
never allowing You to see
the frustrations going on inside of me.
I know You'll be satisfied with the product I can give—
it's foolproof, it's a mask, it's the life that I live.
Are You happy with this picture,
does it make me easy to love?
Have I tried to deceive You,
have I been as peaceful as a dove?
There's just one problem in this mask
I've worn for You—it's full of tiny holes,
and the truth is sifting through.

Revelation Of A Miracle

The revelation of a miracle is appearing in the sky—
The coming of Your Son is drawing nigh.
I'm not ready for the presence of the Everlasting One,
not ready for His true life of flesh and blood.
Oh, I can talk to Him beyond the clouds,
drink in His presence from the look in someone's eyes—
but I don't think I'm ready for that final surprise.
You know I love You, Lord,
and I've given You everything I have to give—
but I need a few more days just to live—
on this earth, that is.

You've made me so happy here,
don't You want me to give some of that away—
spread just a bit more of Your love
before You come to stay?
The book of Revelation, yes, I know it's true.
I believe that everything You've said You will do.
I can feel Your soft petals of wisdom
and warm drops of love—but Jesus,
I can feel them right here with You remaining above.
Still, when it comes right down to the final day
I know I'll be ready, and I'll come running.
You know I wouldn't want to miss the revelation
of a miracle—Your Second Coming.

Doubting

Did I come doubting before Your throne
and expect that You would make me Your own?
Did I doubt the joy of an answered prayer—
did I think it a coincidence or the promise of Your care?
Did I doubt Your love when I was feeling weak,
when my mind was gone, when I could not speak?
Did I doubt that You could heal a broken heart
before it fell apart?
I doubted maybe a thousand things—
countless times I lost my wings.
Afraid to fly, I doubted Your strength.
You knew I was weak.
You made me think.
You allowed me to believe that I had a right to doubt,
when I so bluntly left You out.
Well, You never doubted me,
nor did You interfere with the lesson I was learning,
with my life upside down and my world never turning.
Doubting is not so easy for me now—
I've been caught up in the miracle of believing.

A Spirit
Of Worth

Did I regret that I made you feel worthwhile?
Would I have wanted to miss your happiest smile?
It took a lot of time and effort for you to believe
that you were worth the world
and not just some cast-off weed.
I see you've made it to the top,
but now you're looking down and you're likely to fall
if your eyes remain fixed on the ground.

You're letting human weakness appear in the globe
of your new lifestyle, and you're wondering
if it was worth the time and the pain
to set your sights on a higher plain.
Your life was needed—
because through your eyes you can love the world
and, much to your surprise,
the world will love you in return—
to value yourself is the most important lesson
you have to learn.

Another Phase Of Love

If I could take on your hurts and suffer your falls,
I would do so—for I am part of you.
If I could take away the pain
and still your frenzied mind,
I would give up everything else
just to see peace in your spirit.
You see, you've given life to me in the dying hours
before I could see the dawn.
You built a structure so strong in my heart
that it stands despite the turmoil and the grief.
When I see you coming to me, I'll draw on some
of the strong particles you've created in my soul
and use them to comfort your spirit—
and once again you will be whole.
For we are part of each other,
and the strong will strengthen the weak—
together we are on the brink of another phase of love.

You Touched Me

Could time possibly erase
the warm, contented feeling I had with you?
I could drift maybe a million or more miles away,
but your touch would still be there.
Because you touched my life, I learned to care.
You brought many things into my world;
some were very special and good,
and some were made of confusion—but I understood.
We grew together, you and me,
and then you touched me with serenity.
We laughed together, and you touched me with joy;
we cried together, and you touched me with grief—
and now, somehow, I stare in unbelief
at the whole person I have become.
In your own personal way you taught me so much
by just reaching out with your very special touch.

Love's Journey

If in turning love inward I happen to drown in my tears,
I will have nothing left to fill the lonely years.
If I hide my love behind the world,
I am a useless statue bound in a wall of glass.
I have to be willing to give up my life
in order that someone else might live;
and until I can reach that place,
I haven't even started to run the race—
for love is a journey into a land of promise.
The beginning is rocky,
and there is no room for a doubting Thomas.
Determination to love those who cannot love you back
could break your spirit or even cause you to lose track
of the good things in your life.
There will be no lonely years for you, though,
if you can put together your heart and soul
and prod them to love beyond your control—
for at the end of the journey
only one question will be asked,
"I have loved you—did you love me back?"

Success Of The Cypress

Lyrics of love are falling from the cypress trees.
Can't you see them?
The trees are all a different shape,
bent with years of weathered compassion.
They are not disappointed
because they stand a bit stooped—
I can see above their top branch,
they're not ashamed that they have drooped.
Oh, they are wise with all their years
of twisting and bending.
They may have lived through more agony
than you or I will ever see,
but don't you know
that they are successful in displaying their ability?
They stand proud, silhouetted against God's sky—
He was not critical because they did not grow so high.

He just poured out a little more love
to ease the bending of their limbs.
They look as though they're running
along the coastline, hand-in-hand with God.
He took them in their shrunken state
and made them more beautiful than I can believe—
Oh, God, all their failures are showing,
but their success is more than I can even perceive.
People come from miles away
to look upon their beauty—
You knew it would be that way.
You bent them with the love of Your hand
into their only perfection—
the fierce winds to withstand.